Options Trading:

How to Increase Your Income at Low Risk

© Copyright 2018 by All rights reserved.

The follow eBook is reproduced below with the goal of providing information that is as accurate and reliable as possible. Regardless, purchasing this eBook can be seen as consent to the fact that both the publisher and the author of this book are in no way experts on the topics discussed within and that any recommendations or suggestions that are made herein are for entertainment purposes only. Professionals should be consulted as needed prior to undertaking any of the action endorsed herein.

This declaration is deemed fair and valid by both the American Bar Association and the Committee of Publishers Association and is legally binding throughout the United States.

Furthermore, the transmission, duplication or reproduction of any of the following work including specific information will be considered an illegal act irrespective of if it is done electronically or in print. This extends to creating a secondary or tertiary copy of the work or a recorded copy and is only allowed with express written consent from the Publisher. All additional right reserved.

The information in the following pages is broadly considered to be a truthful and accurate account of facts and as such any inattention, use or misuse of the information in question by the reader will render any resulting actions solely under their purview. There are no scenarios in which the publisher or the original author of this work can be in any fashion deemed liable for any hardship or damages that may befall them after undertaking information described herein.

Additionally, the information in the following pages is intended only for informational purposes and should thus be thought of as universal. As befitting its nature, it is presented without assurance regarding its prolonged validity or interim quality. Trademarks that are mentioned are done without written consent and can in no way be considered an endorsement from the trademark holder.

Table of Contents

Introduction 1

Chapter 1: All About Options 3

Chapter 2: Understanding Risk 14

Chapter 3: Create Your Own Options Trading Plan 23

Chapter 4: Technical Indicators 34

Chapter 5: Options Trading Strategies to Try 42

Chapter 6: Binary Options 57

Chapter 7: Mistakes to Avoid 66

Conclusion 74

Introduction

Congratulations on purchasing Options Trading: How to Increase Your Income at Low Risk and thank you for doing so. Trading options successfully is all about forming a plan that works for you and then developing the mental fortitude to stick with it even when you are in the heat of the moment and your emotions are telling you to double down on a sure thing. While this is certainly easier said than done, this book will provide you with the tools you need to ensure that you come out ahead in the grand scheme of things.

The following chapters will discuss everything you need to know about options trading, starting with the details explaining what exactly options are in the first place. Next, you will learn about the many types of risk you will need to keep in mind in order to trade options effectively as well as how to build a trading plan that will minimize it as much as possible. You will also learn about various technical indicators to be on the lookout for along with options trading strategies to try. Finally, you will learn about the unique possibilities provided by binary options as well as common options trading mistakes to avoid.

Options Trading

There are plenty of books on this subject on the market, thanks again for choosing this one! Every effort was made to ensure it is full of as much useful information as possible, please enjoy!

Chapter 1:

All About Options

In many ways, options are just like bonds or stocks, which means they are securities which can be traded with the hopes of making a profit based on the direction the asset related to the security moves. Options differ from both stocks and bonds in that when you purchase one, you are purchasing the ability to choose whether or not you want to interact with the relevant asset at a specific price point for a specific length of time. This means that if the market doesn't behave as you expect it to, you have the ability to walk away while only losing a fraction of what you would if you had purchased the related asset directly.

While this may sound complicated, in reality, this same process is used every day when individuals who are interested in buying a home negotiate a price with a homeowner who is interested in selling their home and come to an agreement on a price, but then have to wait for the buyer's home loan from a bank to go through. From that point on, it doesn't matter if the market improves dramatically in the interim, the price is locked in for a set amount of time for the buyer to act on, or not, as they deem fit. The buyer in this scenario is protected from unexpected market turns by having the option to buy or pass, just like those buying options based on the stock market.

Using options effectively

Options are primarily used in two different ways, as a type of insurance and for speculative purposes. If you like the idea of testing yourself against the realities of the market, then you may be interested in speculative options in which you try and guess the amount of movement that a specific underlying stock is going to move in a set period of time. As options are frequently traded on margin, even small movements in underlying prices can lead to huge gains or significant losses.

On the other hand, options can be used as a type of insurance on other, riskier investments as they can be purchased at the buy-in price for a risky underlying stock that you believe has the potential to either increase dramatically or decrease significantly. With the right option in place you can weather any uncertainty as if the bottom drops out from underneath the asset then you will still have a sale price that will at least prevent you from losing any investment capital in the interim.

While the chapters in this book are going to primarily focus on stock options, it is important to keep in mind that options trading is available for a wide variety of additional assets as well. Regardless of what type of asset is being optioned, all types of options are classified as either calls (buy orders) or puts (sell orders). From there, each call can be said to be short (expiring in hours, days or minutes) and long (expiring in months or years). Those who are interested in trading as opposed to investing are likely going to want to consider going short while those who are interested in long-term investing may want to consider long equity anticipation securities.

You will also want to keep in mind the two main different types of options, European and American. Despite the names, the differences in the two come from the freedom purchasing an option gives the holder. American options can be exercised from the point they are purchased to the point they expire. Meanwhile, European options can only be exercised right at the moment they expire which makes them the riskier of the two by a fair margin. Both American and European options fall under the classification of vanilla options which means they have standard rates and time limits while exotic options can vary based on a wide variety of criteria which makes them best avoided by beginners.

Besides the options themselves, options traders are also classified based on their propensity to buy (holders) or sell (writers). Writers and holders then typically specialize in either puts or calls. In every trade, the holder will always have more power than the writer as if the holder decides to act on the option the writer has to sell, even if it isn't in their best interest to do so in the moment. Furthermore, if holders find themselves in a scenario where their plan doesn't appear to be coming together they can then easily walk away and minimize their losses at the very least.

Other terms to know

The first step towards trading like the professionals is going to be having a general idea what it is they are talking about which means a short vocabulary lesson is in order. Master the following phrases and you will be on your way to sounding like an expert, at the very least.

Premium – The total amount of value that an option has including its relative level of volatility, time value, strike price, intrinsic value and underlying stock price.

Time Value - Time value can easily be thought of as the amount of time left until the option in question expires. The greater the time value, the more the option is worth

Volatility - The greater the amount of volatility an underlying stock has, the more likely it is to change between now and when any related options expire. The greater the time value, the higher the volatility, though a decreased time value will not necessarily decrease volatility with all underlying stocks.

The money – The money is used in different contexts when it comes to options trading when it comes to discussing how an underlying stock is doing. An underlying stock is "in the money" if it is above the strike price at the moment, "out of the money" if it is currently below the strike price and "at the money" if it is currently sitting at the strike price.

Listed - Options that are traded on a national exchange are said to be listed. The benefits of listed options include that they are clearly marked with expiration dates as well as strike prices so even new options traders can have a clear idea of what is going on. Listed vanilla options almost always include 100 shares of the underlying stock the option is related to.

Trading out – If you are the writer on an option and the holder exercises it at a price that you feel it could do better than, then you can buy it back from them and recreate the option in hopes of getting a better deal. This is what is referred to as trading out and it is the outcome for a vast majority of all options trades. Somewhere around 10 percent of all trades are exercised completely, 50 percent are traded out and the remainer expire uselessly.

Exercise – When the terms of your option become favorable enough that you are interested in acting on it then you exercise the option to purchase or sell the underlying stock related to the option.

Strike Price – The price of the underlying stock at the moment you purchase either a call or a put is referred to as the strike price.

Intrinsic value - If an underlying stock price is current in the money then the difference between the current price of the stock and the strike price can be considered its intrinsic value. Value is discussed in greater detail in a later chapter.

Influences on options

Before you get to the point where you are regularly investing in options, it is important that you have a clear idea of the various influences that come together in order to generate the value that a particular option ends up with. This price is ultimately a combination of many different things including volatility, related interest rates, time value, intrinsic value and, of course, the value of any underlying stock. This means that if you are ever curious if a specific option is going to be the right option for you, then you will need to know its theoretical value as well as the value of any premiums or profits that it might ultimately generate. In this instance, a premium is the guaranteed value that you can expect to get from an option while the theoretical value is what the option is likely going to be worth based on current market signs. Influences to watch include the following.

Underlying stock price: When determining if a given option is a good deal or not, the first thing you are going to want to check is the price of any underlying stock. While the numbers most likely won't match up completely, the option and its underlying stock are always going to move in the same direction as one another. While this movement is thus subject to all of the ups and downs as the stock in question, this will naturally leave it subject to specific patterns as well. As such, if you see that the price of the underlying stock is rising or falling it is a safe bet that the related options are going to do the same thing.

Intrinsic value: The amount of value that a specific option intrinsically holds is the amount that you can count on it to retain no matter what. As the value of an option decreases the closer it gets to its expiration date, the intrinsic value can be thought of the amount of value that will be left over when all the time value is removed. To find the intrinsic value of a call option you will want to start with the current price of the underlying stock before dividing by the difference between the current price and the strike price. With put options, you will find the intrinsic value by taking the difference between the stock price and the strike price and then dividing by the result by the current stock price.

The results from either of these equations will allow you to get a general idea of the type of results you can expect if you exercised the option at its current state and time. For example, if the price of a given stock was sitting at $34.80, then any of the options that were purchased at $30 would have an intrinsic value of $4.80 which is the difference between the purchase price and the current price. Likewise, if you placed a call at $30, then it would worth -$4.80 with an intrinsic value of $0 because the intrinsic value can never be negative.

Time value: The time value of a given option represents the likelihood that it is going to ultimately be worth more that its current intrinsic value at some point before it expires worthlessly. To find the time value of your chosen option, you will need to start by taking the intrinsic value and subtracting out the current value of the option. The greater the result, the greater the chance that the option is going to be profitable before everything is said and done. Generally speaking, options will keep around 70 percent of their value for the first half of their total expiration period before losing it all rapidly in the back half.

It is also important to understand that time value can be directly influenced by the volatility that the underlying stock may be experiencing as well as well as predictions that concern its expiration timeframe as well. The closer an option is to expiring, the more stable it will be, simply because it has less time to change prior to expiring when compared to its contemporaries.

Volatility: Compared to the influencing factors listed above, volatility is much more subjective overall, which is why it is crucial that it is correctly measured when you do take the time to consider it. While it can be difficult to pin down at first, there are plenty of free online sources that will allow you to check your work. Additionally, there are numerous different types of volatility you may need to consider, though the two that tend to influence option price the most are implied volatility and historical volatility.

Historical volatility is a measure of the level of volatility the underlying stock has experienced most recently as well as across the charts for previous weeks, or months if the timeframe is longer. Historical volatility is crucial as it allows you to determine if the current level of movement is par for the course or indicative of the start of a new trend. Implied volatility allows you to determine how volatile the underlying stock is in the moment.

Chapter 2:

Understanding Risk

Risk is at the heart of all types of investment as without it there would be no need for reward. As such, options trading is risky at the best of times, even for those who might be considered experts and certainly for those who are still new to the field. Luckily, there are certainly ways to mitigate that risk as many of the major pitfalls of options trading have been well documented by those who have come before. What's more, they have also been distilled down and classified so that all you need to do is memorize the types of risk outlined below in order to ensure that you do your best to not let it intrude on your trading success.

When it comes time to place any successful trade, it is important to always consider three things, besides the obvious, beforehand. First, you will need to understand how much the price is likely to change between now and when you plan on allowing the option to expire. Second, you will need to consider the level of volatility that the underlying stock is likely to experience in that time as well as how much it has experienced recently. Finally, if you are buying options then you will also need to consider the direction the market is currently moving as well as how much of a hurry it seems to be to get there when compared to the length of the option in question.

However, if you are generating puts then you are going to be primarily concerned with the direction the market is moving in along with the level of volatility of the underlying stock. In this scenario, the amount of time the option has doesn't play as much of a factor when it comes to ensuring you see a maximum level of return on your investments.

Understanding the level of risk is important because most trading strategies are looking for either a positive level of risk to a given underlying stock's trend or a one that is negative. Furthermore, some underlying stocks are always going to be more lucrative in one type of situation or another, which is why it is important to find the perfect time to strike to ensure you maximize your profits. Additionally, it is important to note that just because a risk analysis comes back negative, this in no way means that success is guaranteed. The odds are going to be in your favor, yes, but the market is finicky, and success is practically never assured.

When it comes to determining the potential risks for groups of stocks all at once, you will need to determine the net risk values for the group as a whole, this can be done by simply adding the risk value of each portion of the trade together. This will allow you to determine your next best course of action and maximize the potential for reward versus risk. As such, having a clearer understanding of the various types of risk and what it means for your next trade will also make it easier for you to find the types of trades that naturally line up with your overall tolerance for risk.

Delta: When it comes to options trading, Delta can be thought of as the amount of risk that you take on when you buy into an underlying stock that is likely to move before the option expires. If the underlying stock is currently resting at the strike price, then it has a resting Delta of .5. If this is the case, then you can safely assume that if the underlying stock moves 1 point then the option will move .5 points in the same direction. The call option can sit anywhere between -1 and 1 with the delta on a call sitting between -1 and 0 and the delta on a put resting between 0 and 1.

The delta of a given option should always be the first thing you look to when it comes to deciding if a particular trade is going to be in your favor or ultimately work against you. Additionally, it is going to be the most useful when it can be factored into decisions surrounding puts as you will always want the underlying stock price to move one way or another to ensure a profit from these types of options while also ensuring that the movement isn't so great that it upsets the market entirely.

You can get an overall idea of a given stock's delta by looking at the historical data for the underlying stock in question. This can be done by looking at the historical strike price when compared to put prices along the same time. When measuring delta, it is important to understand that cheaper options are going to typically have lower deltas because they measure how likely the option is to remain profitable at the point of its expiration. As a general rule, you will want to avoid deltas of .4 or .5 (-.4, -.5) as the odds of a trade ending in your favor are small enough to make them rarely worth the trouble.

Vega: Vega is the type of risk that measures how volatile the underlying asset is compared to the market as a whole. Vega can be difficult to accurately determine at points, simply because it is possible to change despite the fact that the price of the asset it points to remained neutral during the same period. As such, making a successful options trade doesn't mean being able to avoid vega completely, it means understanding how to take advantage of it regardless of the level of volatility that is in play.

Options will either respond positively or negatively to an increase in vega, with those that respond positively being labeled "long volatility" options and those that respond negatively being labeled "short volatility" options. Long volatility options tend to have a positive vega while short volatility options have a negative vega. Meanwhile, neutral options won't have any vega risk one way or the other. Additionally, the greater amount of time an option has prior to expiration, the greater their overall volatility and thus their greater amount of vega as well.

For example, if a $4 option is currently connected to an underlying stock that is trading for $90, then that option can be said to have a vega of .1 which would give it 20 percent overall volatility. If the overall level of volatility, then increases by an additional 1 percent then it would increase the overall price of the option to $4.10. The shorter the amount of time the option has left, the greater the amount of increase the change will cause as it becomes less and less likely that the stock will stabilize again prior to the expiration of the option.

Theta: Theta is essentially the measure of the rate at which the time left on a given option is decreasing when compared to the amount of time left prior to its expiration overall. The theta for a given option can result in either a positive or a negative number and it starts to drop the second an option is bought. The total price of the option will decrease at an increasing rate in direct proportion to the amount of time that is left between the moment it is purchases and the moment it expires. As long as the delta exceeds the theta then you can expect to make money on the trade. However, if the Delta drops to a point that the theta exceeds it then the option is profitable for the writer instead.

As an example, if an option has a Theta of .014 then it going to be worth 1.4 cents less in 24 hours than it is right now.

Any put will always have a negative theta and all calls have positive thetas. This stands to reason because puts are worth the most the moment they are created, and calls are worth the most the moment before they expire; either way, this is always going to be the point where the potential difference between the starting and ending price is going to be the most austere.

As such, Theta is always in flux, and the intensity of its fluctuations are only going to get more extreme as the option inches closer and closer to its expiration date. This is one of the reasons that buyers are more attracted to long-term options than those with shorter timeframes as the theta is going to be less of a factor in these instances. Thea is especially important if you are planning to make a trade based on the assumption that the market is going to retain a neutral state for any true length of time. When this is not the case then theta can be largely mitigated as long as you factor it into each of your trades appropriately.

Gamma: If delta measures the change an option experiences in relation to its underlying stock, then gamma measures the amount of variation the delta sees over the life span of the option in question. Gamma naturally increases the closer the option and the underlying stock grow to one another and decrease if the stock moves past the strike point. The greater the amount of gamma a specific option has, the greater chance for profit, and the greater chance for risk as well. Gama tends to increase more rapidly as the option moves closer to its expiration date. If you need to know much this increase is going to increase per fraction of the remaining timeframe then you can simply find the gamma of the gamma.

For example, if you purchase a stock that is trading at around $50 per share, along with its related option that is currently trading at $2, with a delta of .4 and a gamma rating of .1, then if the stock rose by $1 per share then the delta would increase by 10 percent, just as the gamma predicted. When the volatility is low, and the gamma is greater than .5, then the option will be of a price that is great than the initial strike price. If the gamma drops below .5, then it is likely below the price point as well. In general, you can expect gamma to retain a greater degree of stability when it comes to highly volatile underlying stocks as opposed to those with a lower level of volatility overall.

Rho: Rho is a level of risk that rarely comes into play as it relates to the level of risk surrounding the probability of the interest rates of a specific option changing and altering the underlying stock price in a negative fashion. In general, interest rates and call prices increase at the same time while puts will decrease in value. The reverse is also true and put prices will increase when interest rates decrease. Rho will be at its highest amount when the underlying stock price is equal or greater than that of the option that is being purchased or sold. Rho value is always negative for puts while calls always have a positive value. Rho value is at its most important when options trading is being used as a long-term investment strategy.

Chapter 3:
Create Your Own Options Trading Plan

Make a personalized trading plan

When it comes to making sure that you are able to manage something more than avoiding losing your shirt when you start trading options for the first time, it is important that you start by assessing your current situation. You are going to want to determine what your personalized trading plan looks like and how you can likely go about maximizing your strengths while minimizing your weaknesses. You are going to need to do more than simply making a plan, however, you will also need to commit to following through on the plan even when you are in the heat of the moment and your emotions are telling you to make different choices instead.

Know yourself: The first step to creating a reliable trading plan is to know your personal strengths as well as your weaknesses. The first place to start with this assessment is with the strength of your abilities when it comes to choosing successful trades recently as well as overall in your trading career. With these specifics in mind, you are going to then be able to determine how much risk you are comfortable with taking on in order to see the types of results you are looking for. If you don't like what you come up with, you can either change the amount you hope to generate as profit, the amount of risk you are comfortable with or the amount you have to invest right off the bat. The overall result is always going to be a result of these three factors.

Additionally, it is important to consider how well you can control your emotions, even when things aren't going your way and how likely you are to stick to your plan once you have created it. After all, it doesn't matter how airtight your plan is if you don't have the emotional and mental fortitude to stick with it once things stop going your way. If you feel as though you are naturally in control of yourself at all times, then you will already be well on your way to improving your overall trade results. If not, you will need to favor strategies that allow you to take your emotional nature into account. Failing to do so is simply asking for trouble.

Consider your goals: It will also be important to consider your goals when it comes to options trading as these can easily affect the ultimate strategy that you choose to pursue. This could be something safe, such as keeping your initial trading capital intact no matter what, or it could be something with a greater amount of risk and potential reward. The specifics themselves don't matter, what matters is that you take the time to clearly identify your plan and then stick with it once it has been instigated. When choosing your goals, keep in mind that your trades don't exist in a vacuum, be sure to accurately consider any external factors when in the planning stage.

The amount you can you afford to lose: Finally, when deciding on how much you are going to spend on your new options trading adventure, it is important to keep in mind that you should never invest more than you can afford to lose. If you decide to invest money that you need for more pressing matters in a volatile market, then you will never be able to look at your investment rationally and will always be concerned about protecting those funds. It is also important to factor in how long you anticipate holding the investment for as the more time you have, the more you will be able to let loose and take risks as you will have plenty of time to correct them if things don't work out.

Choose your moments carefully: Once you have a general idea of what your investment levels are going to be, the next thing you will want to consider is how these numbers will actively translate into successful trades via finding the right entry and exit points to support your gradually forming plan. Prior to entering into any short-term trade, it is extremely important that you know when you are going to be willing to walk away either because you have made an adequate profit or because you can't realistically afford to go any further into the red. The urge to stay in wring every last cent out of a successful trade is natural in relatively new traders and is often misleading as overtime it is likely to cause you to lose out much more than you will ever gain.

When it comes to choosing the right exit points you will always want to focus on the limits of your tolerance for risk and avoid changing the exit point once the trade has started, no matter what. On the other hand, when it comes to choosing profitable entry points you will never want to make a move on a trade that doesn't mesh with your own natural tolerance for risk. It doesn't matter how good of a deal a trade might be if it falls outside the level of risk that you are comfortable with then you will never be able to act on it as effectively as possible.

Once you know the types of trades you are looking for in general then you will be able to look into various types of strategies that support those types of trades. There are countless different strategies available, as long as your plan is profitable then you should easily be able to find one that fits your plan like a glove.

Dedicate yourself to it: While you are going to want to test your plan first to ensure that it is working at, or above, 50 percent effectiveness, it is important to commit yourself to it the way a machine would commit itself to a specific task. The only way you will ever be able to rely on any results that you gather will be if you can reliably count on yourself to stick to the plan no matter what, even during moments when you are having a long run of bad luck and it feels as though the rules of your plan are only holding you back from reaching your true potential. This level of dedication is certainly hard to reach, but if you manage to do so then you will see far more profit in the long-run than you would ever see by going off book when your emotions tell you it is the right thing to do.

Check your results

In order to determine if your trading system is as effective as possible, it is important to keep track of your trades and analyze the results about once a month. It is important that you don't overanalyze your results as otherwise a handful of good (or bad) trades can throw the entire average off and cause you to move forward in a less than optimal manner.

The metrics that you are going to find to be the most helpful are going to vary based on your personal trading style. If you prefer high risk/high reward trades, then you are going to be more interested in total net profit while if you prefer to avoid as much risk as possible then your successful trade percentage is going to be more useful. Regardless, it is vital that you review and thoroughly understand a wide variety of different performance metrics related to your plan or to your system before determining if it is time to try something new.

Know yourself

Instead of being in a rush to look into how effective your plan is or setting daily trading goals that are, frankly, completely unrealistic, especially so early on, you will want to make a point of sticking to the plan that you created and keeping detailed notes on every single trade that you make, what the results are and what all of the relevant details turned out to be. To determine the metrics that are most relevant to your overall success, you are going to want to first ask yourself what type of trader you are.

If you are someone who is always hunting for big risks and bigger rewards, then you will be much better served by finding out how successful you have been overall in a given time period (starting with one month of data) as opposed to the number of successful or unsuccessful trades. On the other hand, if your overall number of trades is very low because you only make extremely safe moves, then you will want to ensure that each trade you make is as profitable as possible.

Create a performance report

You will use the data you have recorded to create a performance report relating to the trading plan or strategy that you are currently using. This report will let you take a critical look at the rules you are using the determine your trades and determine how it is likely going to continue performing over a set period of time. Creating a performance report will help you understand the historical volatility of your plan.

When getting started with a performance report, the best place to start is by creating a summary of the metrics that you have collected over the past few weeks. Ideally, you will want to include information on every trade that was completed, if it was a put or a call, the time and data it occurred and the results of the trade overall. While it will be tempting, you will find that avoiding daily data will make it easier to see the forest for the trees.

Keeping a broader focus will help you determine not just the amount you are making overall but also why certain trades failed while others succeeded. Taking the time to do so can make it easier for you to turn fluke instances of success into patterns instead. When it comes to determining your performance, you are also going to want to check in on your performance graph which can be found under Tools on the TradeKing site. This graph can either be seen as a bar graph or as what is known as an equity curve, though the bar graph will be illustrative enough to immediately tell you what you need to know.

Specific measurable variables

Your performance report will likely contain reams and reams of data, so much so that finding a clear starting point can be difficult. Do yourself a favor and focus on the following, as the rest essential just reconfirms what you will already know.

Total net profit: Your total net profit is the overall monetary success or failure of the system or plan in question. It can be found by including the total gross loss for the period, including commission costs and subtracting it from the total amount made on every successful trade. While this is a great way to broadly determine if you are on the right track, it can be deceptive as well. This is because it does not explain how often the system was successful, just the overall results.

Profit Factor: The profit factor can be found if you take the total amount of any gross profits before dividing them by the total amount of any gross losses, again including any fees that may be included across the amount of time being studied. If your results are 1 or above, then congratulations your system or plan is profitable, otherwise, you will need to rethink your strategy. The resulting number is indicative of how many units of profit you can broadly expect versus 1 theoretical unit of risk. The bigger the number the bigger the difference between various wins and losses.

Net profit trade average: The average amount of net profit per trade is how much you are generally going to profit from each trade based on your history of successful trades in the past. To determine this average, you need to take the total amount of profit you have seen thus fare and divide that by the complete number of trades you have completed. Again, there is no ideal number, you just want something that is positive and works within the confines of the goals you have set. When determining this number, you want to leave out any extreme outlier trades that were far from normal for either better or worse as they will skew your data and can make even successful plan appear to be performing poorly.

Chapter 4:

Technical Indicators

Technical indicators

As the name implies, technical indicators are used in options trading as a way to determine trends as well as potential turning points in the price of underlying stocks. When used correctly, they can accurately predict movement cycles as well as determine when the most profitable time to buy or sell is going to be.

Technical indicators are typically calculated based on the price pattern of a derivative or stock. Relevant data includes closing price, opening price, lows, highs and volume. Indicators typically take the data regarding a stock's price from the past few periods depending on the charts the analyst favors and use it to generate a trend that will show what has been happening with a specific stock as well as what is likely to happen next.

There are two primary types of technical indicators, leading and lagging. Lagging indicators are used to determine if a new trend if forming or if the underlying stock is currently moving within an expected range through the use of existing data. If the lagging indicator points to a strong trend, then there is a better than 50 percent chance the trend will continue moving forward. Unfortunately, they are not especially useful when it comes to determining pullbacks or rally points that may appear in the future.

Alternately, leading indicators tend to come into play when traders need to predict a likely future price point when it is currently unclear if the current price is going to crash or rally. They tend to manifest as momentum indicators which help to determine the strength of the movement of the current trend which will help to determine if the trend is going to continue or reverse. As no trend will continue forever, the momentum indicator will allow you to determine how long of a timeframe your options should be in to ensure that you get out before the disruption begins.

Leading indicators are also useful if you find yourself needing to determine if the price of a specific stock has reached a point where it is unsustainable as this means a slowdown in the price is forthcoming. As overbought or oversold stocks experience a pullback when a slowdown occurs, knowing when this type of movement is coming can thus be supremely useful for several different trading strategies.

Each indicator is useful in specific situations which means that both are equally important when it comes to determining the trends that are forming around the underlying stocks in question. As a general rule, you are going to want to use at least three different indicators to get a feel for the market at all times.

Moving average convergence divergence indicator

The moving average convergence divergence (MACD) indicator is an oscillating indicator that typically moves between a zero point and a centerline. If it generates an especially high value when used this is indicative that the underlying stock in question is quite likely going to be overbought while if it is an extremely low value, then it indicates the stock is likely going to be oversold.

MACD charts are based on a combination of 3 different exponential moving averages (EMA). These averages can be based on any period, though the most common are the

12-26-9 chart. The first part of this chart is generally listed as the 12-day and 26-day EMA. The 12-day EMA is the faster of the two.

A combination of faster and slower EMAs makes it easier for traders to accurately gauge the current level of momentum that the trends they are watching are expressing. When the 26-day EMA is below the 12-day EMA then the underlying stock is experiencing an uptrend while the reverse is true if the 26-day is higher instead. If the 12-day EMA is also increasing faster than the 26-day, then the uptrend is going to become more pronounced as well. If the 12-day EMA starts to slow, and the two EMAs start to close on one another, then the momentum of the trend is likely starting to fade signaling that a reversal could soon be in effect.

The MACD utilizes these two EMAs by comparing the difference between the two and plotting it for easier usage. If the pair of EMAs ends up being the same, then the MACD works out to be 0. If the 26-day is below the 12 days, then the MACD will be positive, and if the 26-day is above then the MACD will be negative. If the MACD is positive, then the difference between the two will drive it away from the centerline; while if it is negative then the difference will drive it away from zero instead.

While the MACD doesn't provide all that much more detail when compared to the standard moving average, its value increases dramatically when it is used in conjunction with the 9-day EMA as well. The 9-day EMA differs from the other EMAs in that it is based on the MACD line as opposed to the stock price. As a result, this EMA then smooths out the MACD line to make its results more useful overall.

On certain occasions, you will also find a use for the MACD histogram which visualizes the difference between the MACD line and the 9-day EMA line. If the MACD line cross through the 9-day EMA line at a point higher than 0, then the upcoming trend is likely to be bearish, otherwise it is likely to be bullish. If the charted histogram generates a number of descending peaks, then this will be known as a negative divergence, while a positive divergence forms in the opposite way.

If a negative divergence occurs, then it is a strong sign that any positive trends that are currently in place will be reversing sooner than later. This will remain true in all scenarios, even if the underlying stock price seems to be in the midst of a very strong positive trend. The same is true in an opposite sense for positive divergence and negative trends. These signals can become somewhat muddy when the price trades at the range for a prolonged period of time which is why it is important to always use multiple indicators to avoid seeing false signals.

Average directional index

The average directional index acts as a type of guide that confirms the signals generated by other technical indicators you may choose to use. Once a trend is identified, the average directional index can determine its relative strength. The average directional index is a combination of both the positive and negative directional indicators which track upward and downward trends respectively. The average directional index then combines them into a unified way to determine the relative strength of a trend.

The average directional index is an oscillating indicator with a range between 0 and 100. Zero indicates a flat trend with virtual no volatility while 100 indicates that a given stock is moving practically straight up or down with a large degree of volatility. This indicator only measures the relative strength of the trend, it will not tell you which direction it is likely to move in.

The average directional index typically tops out at around 60 as most trends that reach this level of strength tend to only manifest during long recessions or very long bullish market runs. Generally speaking, any value greater than 40 is considered quite strong while anything lower than 20 is within trading range. The average directional signal is good for several different signals, starting with those given off if the trends drops from somewhere north of 40 to somewhere south. When this occurs, it is a strong indicator that the trend is starting to slow which is bad for most strategies which means you are going to want to start closing out your trades when you notice it appearing.

If you watch a trend go from around 20 to above 30 then you can safely assume that the sideways movement that has recently been plaguing the market is about to come to an end as long as a new trend can come along to supersede it. You will also want to take not of the point where the negative directional index and the positive directional index meet. If the positive index crosses above the negative index, then the market is sending bullish signals and if the opposite is true then the market is sending positive signals.

Regardless of how strong the trends you uncover may be up front, it is highly recommended that you never make any trades based on just one indicator alone. Three is the magic number when it comes to ensuring that what you aren't seeing in the current market trend is more than just a fluke and is something that you can legitimately expect to act on with some degree of certainty.

Chapter 5:

Options Trading Strategies to Try

While throwing yourself whole hog into the options market means taking in a great deal of information in a short period of time, there are plenty of strategies to use that are likely to improve your returns and reduce your risk as greatly as possible.

Start strategies

Covered call: Also known as the buy-write strategy, this strategy works by purchasing a call on an underlying asset in addition to purchasing the asset itself. To maximize the likelihood of this strategy working out in your favor it is important to create a call in proportion to the position you took on the underlying asset. This strategy is especially useful if you own a separate position in the short-term as well and feel as though the related underlying asset is either going to decrease in value or see only sideways movement during the timeframe that your option is active. If timed correctly, this strategy allows you to ensure you will receive a bonus premium, while also protecting your primary investment in the process. Covered calls are typically used with assets that are purchased on margin, LEAPS and index futures.

Married puts: A married put is an ideal strategy if you have a bullish attitude on the price of a particular underlying asset while also hoping to shore up any potential losses. To make use of this strategy, the first thing you will want to do is to buy into a set amount of an underlying asset while also purchasing a put to cover the same amount. This put will then act as a price floor that will make it easy for you to prevent a loss in case of a sudden price drop. While dropping additional money into a losing proposition is never recommended, adding a married put to a shaky underlying asset you already have in your portfolio is a good way to mitigate potential future risk.

While not the best choice in every situation, if used sparingly, as a cautionary measure, married puts can be a reliable way to improve your overall options trading success. To ensure this always works out in your favor, you will never want to begin a new transaction without having a clear understanding of the risk you are working with beforehand. You will then be able to factor in additional costs more easily and compare the total cost to the amount of risk you are going mitigate as a result. From there it is simply doing the math and choosing the option that makes the most fiscal sense. As an added bonus, married puts help mitigate the potential risk related to early options to exercise as it ensures you always have available shares ready and waiting.

Bull call spread: To utilize this strategy, you will need to begin with a call option that you can purchase at a strike price that will be worth following up on in the future. At the same time, you will want to sell an equal number of calls at a strike price above your starter strike price but within a reasonable distance. Both of these calls will then need to have the same timeframe and underlying asset. This is a great strategy to employ if you are bullish on the strength of a current underlying asset or your research otherwise indicates that the price is likely to increase for the time frame you have chosen.

This strategy also goes by the name vertical credit spread thanks to its mismatched legs. Those that sell close to the money result in a credit spread that includes a positive time value and a net credit. Debit spreads are created if a short option ends further away from the money than the point it started from. Regardless, you can consider this strategy a net buy.

Bear put spread: The bear put spread is similar in practice to the bull call spread, expect that it is used under opposite circumstances. To start, you will need to purchase a pair of put options with differing strike prices, one higher and one lower. You will want to also purchase equal numbers of each, while also ensuring they are set to the same timeframe and related to the same asset. This strategy is especially useful if you have a bearish opinion of the underlying asset as it can easily limit your losses if you judge the market incorrectly. Be cautious when using this strategy, however, as the profits you see are ultimately going to be limited to the difference between the two puts you purchases after transaction fees have been taken into account.

The most profitable time to use a bear put spread is when you plan on short selling an underlying asset but a basic put option isn't really the right choice. You will find them especially useful if you plan on speculating that prices are going to decrease but don't want to employ additional capital just waiting for the worst to happen. When using this strategy, you are thus able to hope for the best while still planning for the worst.

Protective collar: The protective collar strategy can be executed by buying into a put option that is already out of the money. From there, you will then want to write a secondary call option that is based on the same underlying asset and is also out of the money. This strategy is useful if you have already taken a long position on an underlying asset that has seen a number of strong gains in the recent past. Making use of a protective collar then allows you to ensure the current level of profit remains steady while also retaining control of the underlying asset should its positive trend continue.

Utilizing a protective collar is as easy as ensuring the contract for the put option you purchased was at a strike price that is more than likely enough to ensure you retain a majority of the profits you gained through the process. From there, you will be able to fund the collar strategy using the call option you have written as long as you are sure it relates to the specific Digit. This strategy is particularly useful as it allows you to easily maintain your profits while at the same time only increasing your additional costs a minimal amount. Furthermore, this is a great way to move funds about for tax purposes as any option that you roll over does not need to be accounted for until it has been either purchased or expired.

Straddles: The long straddle is especially useful if you believe that the price of an underlying asset is going to move a great deal in a specific direction, but you are unclear as to what direction that will be. As such, you will want to purchase a call as well as a put, both with the same underlying asset, timeframe and strike price. Once the long straddle is up and running you can rest easy you are sure to see a gain as long as the price moves before your options expire.

If you are interested in utilizing a short straddle, you will instead want to sell a call and a put with the same costs, timeframe and underlying asset. Doing so will ensure that you profit from the premium, at the very least, which is useful if you don't expect much movement at all during the timeframe in question. It is important to keep in mind, however, that the odds of success when it comes to this strategy will decrease in direct proportion to the amount the underlying asset ultimately ends up moving, regardless of the direction.

Long strangle: To make use of a long strangle, you will need to purchase a call and a put that is based on the same underlying asset along with the same maturation level. They will need to have different strike prices, however. The strike price for the call should be above the price for the put and both should start at a point that is out of the money. This is an especially useful strategy if you expect the underlying asset to move a good deal but are unclear as to which direction it will choose. When utilized correctly, you will be practically guaranteed to make a profit after the related costs have been taken into account.

Functionally, a strangle is similar to a straddle except that it is often cheaper to execute on as you are buying into options that are already out of the money. As such, you can typically pay as much as 50 percent the cost of a straddle for a strangle which makes it even easier to play both sides of the fence. Typically, a long strangle is more useful than a short straddle because it offers up twice the premium for the same amount of risk.

Butterfly spread: A butterfly spread is a mixture of a bear spread strategy and a more traditional bull strategy which also makes use of a total of 3 strike points. To start with, you will want to purchase a call option at the lowest price possible. From there, you will want to sell two calls at a price that is higher along with a third call that is even higher still. The goal here should be to ensure that a range of potential profits are possible at prices that are within the current trend.

This strategy can be deployed most effectively when your opinion on the current market is completely neutral. Additionally, you should expect the underlying asset to move in your favor, even if you are unsure about the overall level of gains you should expect. This, in turn, means you should strive to keep market volatility as low as possible. The greater the overall level of volatility, the greater the cost to set up this type of strategy. Additionally, it is important to keep in mind that if you are incorrect about the direction of the current trend then the losses with this type of strategy can be substantial.

Iron condor: In order to use the iron condor strategy successfully, you will want to start with a short position along with a long position through the use of a pair of joint strangle strategies that are poised to take full advantage of a low volatility market. One of these strangles should be long while the other should be short and set to the outer strike price. You can also accomplish the same thing using a pair of credit spreads. In this case, the call spread would be above the current market price and the put would be below the current market price.

The iron condor is only advisable when trading using index options as they offer an increased level of volatility that actually comes along with an overall lower increase of risk than if you were going after any of the stocks individually. As such, you are only going to want to release the iron condor if you are supremely confident that the market is going to move the way your research indicates it will as otherwise you stand to leave yourself open to a significant amount of additional risk.

Iron butterfly: To start an iron butterfly you want to use either a long or a short straddle and concurrently either purchase or sell a strangle based on the straddle you chose. While similar to a basic butterfly, this strategy utilizes both calls and puts rather than just one or the other. When done properly it limits the potential for profit or loss to the range of the strike prices that you set. This strategy is best used with options that are out of the money as they allow you to minimize both risk and cost.

Double Diagonal Strategy

To take advantage of the double diagonal strategy, you are going to want to start by running a diagonal put spread at the same time you are running a diagonal call spread. Remember, in a diagonal spread, you want to take a horizontal spread based on time and move the long leg to an alternate strike point. It is called a diagonal spread because the legs do not have the same month.

In a diagonal call spread, you will want to cross a sort call spread with a long calendar spread which means you are going to want to make a move based on time decay. After you have sold off the second call at the first strike point you will have legged yourself into a spread for the short call. This will help you to generate a net credit which means that once you sell the second call you will be making a pure profit. The same theory goes for a diagonal put, though obviously, the specifics are going to be quite different.

Getting started with the double diagonal: As such, you are going to want to get into the habit of making use of the double diagonal spread along with the diagonal put spread to ensure you can take advantage of accelerated time decay as much as possible when dealing with front-month options. This is in direct contrast to the more predictable pace of options waiting in the back month. The strategy works as follows.

1. Begin with an out of the money put at a specific strike price you believe will be profitable with a two-month expiration.

2. Simultaneously sell an out of the money put with another potentially profitable strike price that is going to expire in one month.

3. Simultaneously sell an out of the money call at a specific strike price you believe will be profitable with a two-month expiration.

4. Simultaneously sell an out of the money call with another potentially profitable strike price that is going to expire in one month.

Your goal during this strategy is to choose an underlying stock price that is going to remain between the price of the 30-day put and call. If the price remains above the strike price, then you will want to sell the options that are 30 days out while also selling another round of puts at the initial strike price and selling another call at the second profitable strike price that expires at the same time as the 60-day call. It is important to keep in mind that when you are looking at graphs of this strategy the profit lines are going to never be completely straight as the 60-day options are still open. Straight lines and hard angles are only truly possible if all of the options in the strategy expire at exactly the same time.

While this strategy might sound complicated when explained step by step, it becomes far more manageable if you consider it as a means of profiting from a neutral amount of market movement that is expressed across numerous cycles of expiration.

Proper execution: The most profitable time to make use of this strategy is when the underlying stock is currently sitting somewhere between the longer put strike price and the short call strike price, the closer it is to the exact midpoint between the two, the better as it indicates the strategy is free of any bearish or bullish bias. If the stock remains at this point until the options expire then anything you sold will expire while you will remain free to profit from the resulting premiums to the maximum degree.

In this scenario, the shorter put and the longer call work to minimize the amount of risk you are likely to experience if the underlying stock ends up moving with greater force than you initially anticipated. Furthermore, your goal when using this strategy should also be to generate a net credit, which is not always possible due to the fact that the front-month options are always going to have far less time value than the back-month options. As such, when faced with this scenario then you will always want to go for a net debit instead before then making up the difference by selling an additional set of options assuming the firs expire as planned.

Assuming the front-month options reach a point where the existing trend says they are likely to expire sooner than later then you will want to ensure that the underlying stock price is between the second put and the first call for the best results. Assuming this is the case, you will then want to buy in close to the first pair of options before selling a third put at the second strike price and a third call at the third strike price. This new round of options should all expire at the 60-day expiration date. This part of the strategy is known as rolling out.

Completion: A common habit for many traders is purchasing front-month options when they don't want to deal with options that are going to expire at a disadvantageous time. As such, they are able to prevent having to deal with price swings that occur after the market closes and when it opens again. This means they will aim for underlying stock prices that stay where they started until the remainder of the options expires out of the money. When this occurs, they are then free to pocket the related premiums that come from a properly executed double diagonal. This is what makes the double diagonal preferable to a longer iron condor in many traders' eyes, in this scenario you also get to take the premium related to the short options at the second and third strike price, not just once, but twice.

Covered call: Also called the buy-write strategy, a covered call involves purchasing an underlying asset while also generating a call on the same asset. In order to ensure this strategy works properly it is important to create a call based on how much of the underlying asset you own. This strategy is extremely effective if you own a separate position in the short term and feel that the underlying asset is either going to stay the same or decrease in value in the time frame for the option you created. When done properly, it allows you to generate a bonus premium at the very least. Covered calls are an effective strategy when used with index futures, LEAPS and on funds that are traded via an exchange and purchased on a margin.

Chapter 6:

Binary Options

Binary options are similar to traditional options in many ways except that they ultimately boil down to a basic yes or no question. Instead of worrying about what exact price an underlying stock is going to have, a binary option only cares if it is going to be above one price at the time of its expiration. Traders then make their trades based on if they believe the answer is yes or no. While it may seem simple on its face, it is important that you fully understand the ways in which binary options work, as well as the time frames and markets they work with. It is also important to understand the specific advantages and disadvantages that they have, and which companies are legally allowed to offer binary options for trade.

Binary options are also a great choice for those who are interested in testing the waters of day trading but don't have the significant amount of capital on hand which is required to participate in stock market day trading. This is due to the fact that traditional stock market day trading limits don't apply to binary options which means you can start trading with just $1,000 in your trading account.

When considering binary options, it is also important to keep in mind that binary options are a derivative created by its association with an underlying asset which means they don't give you ownership of that asset in any way. What this means is that there is no way for you to exercise them as a means of obtaining dividends or gaining voting rights, or anything else you might expect from a standard option.

For example, assume you are looking at a binary option for gold that states its price will be greater than $1,450 by 2 pm today. If the market seems to be pointing in that direction, then you will want to purchase the binary option, otherwise, you would want to sell instead. Additionally, assuming that the bid price of the option is $54.50 and the asking price is $56.50 with 30 minutes left until its expiration time. If you decided to buy in at this point you would pay $56.50 and if you sold you would pay $54.50.

If you ultimately decided to buy in and were successful, then you could expect your option to expire with a status of paid and you would make $100, which would be about $40 after fees and the cost were taken into account. If the price doesn't break the target point, however, then the option becomes worthless and you are out the cost you spent to buy it in the first place. As with other options, the price will continue to fluctuate down until the option expires.

One of the nice things about binary options is their reliability, each will either be worth $100 or $0 when the time comes which makes determining costs and potential profits far less complex than with other types of trading. From there, the ask and bid prices are set by traders who are setting their prices based on how likely the option in question is going to come true. The higher the prices, the greater the perceived odds of the option's success. If the price is about half the price of the payout then the odds are considered even and if it is more favorable, then the odds are against the option paying out.

Trading binary options: Binary options can currently be trading on the Nadex exchange, the first and only exchange dedicated to selling binary options legally in the United States. It allows for browser-based trading through its own platform which offers many of the amenities you expect, including real time charts and the latest binary options pricing.

Binary options are also now available on the Chicago Board Options Exchange which can only be accessed via a brokerage account that has already been cleared for binary options trading. Not all brokers are going to offer binary options trading, however, which means if you plan on going down this route then you are going to need to ensure the broker you go with provides the services you are looking for.

Trading through the Nadex costs 90 cents, regardless if you are entering a trade or exiting one. The max fee is capped at $9 per trade. If you hold your trade until it expires then the fees will be taken out at that point. If the trade ends up being out of the money when it expires you will not be charged a fee. Trading via CBOE is handled through specific options brokers who charge a variety of different commission fees.

Binary markets to choose from: While getting set up with a binary options trading account might be more difficult than with some other options, once you are ready to go you will then be free to trade in as many different asset classes as you like. Nadex allows for trading via all the primary indices including S&P 500, Nasdaq 100, Russell 2000 and Dow 30. The UK, German and Japanese indices are also available as are trades in numerous different forex pairs such as AUD/JPY, AUD/USD, EUR/GBP, EUR/JPY, EUR/USD, GBP/JPY, GBP/UDS, USD/CAD, USD/CHF and USD/JPY.

From there, Nadex also offers binary options based on commodity trading including natural gas, crude oil, silver, copper, gold and soybeans. You will also find that the outcome of upcoming news events will see plenty of options. For example, you can purchase binary options based on whether or not you believe that the Federal Reserve is going to announce a decrease in joblessness in the country.

The Chicago Board Options Exchange, on the other hand, offers a variety of binary options that tend to have a smaller overall amount of variance to choose from when compared to other offerings. Additionally, you will typically find that their offerings are not found anywhere else as well. You can also find options that are based on various interpretations of the S&P 500 as well as a volatility option index based around its own volatility index.

Risk and reward: Binary option risk is capped at the cost of the initial trade as the worst thing that will ever happen is that your option expires at 0. The risk is also capped, though it can still offer up significant returns depending on the amount of the initial investment. For example, if you purchase a binary option for $20, that ends up paying out, then you will still make $100 off of it ($80 profit) which means you have a 4:1 reward ratio which is more than you could find if you invested in the related stock directly.

This only works out in your favor to a point, however, as your gains will always top out at $100, no matter how much movement the underlying stock actually experienced. This downside can be mitigated to some extent simply by purchasing multiple options contracts up front.

Binary option trading strategies

Pinocchio strategy: This is a useful strategy to try if you find yourself starring at a candle bar with an extremely long wick and a very small body. This type of bar is commonly known as pin bar but was given its moniker due to the fact that a longer wick is more likely to give off false information. As such, if you come across this scenario and the wick is already extremely long, then you can typically assume that the price of the underlying stock has already moved as far as it can in a specific direction and will be reversing sooner rather than later. As such, you can think of this type of bar as an indicator that you are going to want to start trading against the majority as the trend is likely going to catch up with you if you start ahead of it.

Binary option reversal strategy: This strategy gains its effectiveness from the fact that the market naturally seeks to balance itself which means that any price is bound to eventually turn when confronted with either extreme highs or extreme lows. This means you can easily get a jump on this movement by accurately predicting what is going to happen next. Obviously, in order for this strategy to work out effectively, you are going to need to be able to accurately predict the need for a call or a put based o the situation as it stands with help of the information you have been able to gather so far.

This can be an especially useful strategy during times where the underlying asset is moving quite quickly as the speed at which it moves in one direction is typically a strong indication of when it is going to move back the opposite direction. As the asset movement is likely going to repeat itself eventually, once you can correctly determine the patterns you will be able to more easily tell if and when a specific underlying asset is at its peak, making any decisions you need to make regarding specific binary options far clearer cut.

Trade the News: Buying into binary assets based on information that is going to be revealed by a major source can be a more multifaceted approach than it first appears. At its most basic level, it involves purchasing contracts when good news is forthcoming and then selling when bad news is forthcoming. Unlike other strategies, it is much less of a strict science than it is the art of knowing how people expect the news to go compared to what you may actually be able to discover beforehand.

If you are fairly certain a specific piece of news is going to be released and you aren't sure how the market is going to react to it, then the best way to ensure that you are going to end up making a profit is by setting up boundaries. To set up a bound binary option, all you need to do is pick 2 prices, one on either side of the current price of the underlying asset. As long as the price of the two is less than $50 combined you will still be making a reasonable profit, even after one of them expires at $0. The biggest risk with this strategy is that if the price doesn't move at all then you both binary options are likely to expire at $0, costing you both the entry fees in the process.

Chapter 7:

Mistakes to Avoid

Not avoiding Out of the Money call options: Out of the Money calls options can often feel safe because it follows a traditional pattern of buying low and selling high. Nevertheless, it is a very difficult way to see consistent returns as it still amounts to little more than gambling. Likewise, following this procedure can make it difficult to learn anything as the reasons why an individual option succeeded or failed can be difficult to pinpoint to the uninitiated.

Remember, when you buy an option you need to not only determine what direction the underlying stock is going to move in, you also need to determine when it is going to move. If you judge either poorly then you are out the premium you paid for the option, the price of the commission and you tied up the rest of your investment while the option expired. It is important to understand that just because an underlying stock increased on an Out of the

Money options the amount you see in a return is related to a probability of the underlying stock reaching a strike price.

Ignoring the importance of the delta: Everyone knows that if the delta of the option you are considering is near 1, then you will want to generate calls and if it is near -1 then you will want to generate puts. When it comes to cheap options, however, you will want to choose options with a higher delta as they are more likely to conform with the expectations you might have in relation to the underlying stock which means you will see greater gains when the underlying stock does, in fact, begin to move.

Trading without a clear goal in mind: Even if you are just learning all of the ins and outs of options trading, it is important that you never do any trading without a clear idea of what you hope to gain. Trading without a clear set of goals is a surefire way to lose money, even if you are following a relatively sure thing. If nothing in the market sticks out to you at a given time as something that is worth working towards, then there is no shame in walking away until the market turns around in a favorable direction. Many new traders make the mistake of thinking that they always need to be trading when in reality this is not the case and will often lead to greater losses than it ever will gains. Trying to get blood from a stone benefits no one, set goals early and often, but don't force them if they aren't readily available.

Hanging on too tightly to your starter strategy: The personalized trading strategy that you created in chapter four if you have been following along, is an important step in trading properly, no two ways around it. That doesn't mean that it is the last strategy that you are ever going to need, however, far from it. Your core trading strategy is one that should always be constantly evolving as the circumstances surrounding your trading habits change and evolve as well. What's more, outside of your primary strategy you are going to want to eventually create additional plans that are more specifically tailored to various market states or specific strategies that are only useful in a narrow band of situations. Remember, the more prepared you are prior to starting a day's worth of trading, the greater your overall profit level is likely to be, it is as simple as that.

Making a move without knowing the risks: While from time to time you may come across a potential trade that appears as though it is going to be a sure thing, acting on this hunch without doing your homework first is always going to end in disaster. Before you purchase options or underlying stock it is critical that you look at the trade from all angles which means understanding how likely you are, not just to make a profit on the transaction, but lose everything as well. This is why it is so important to utilize either fundamental or technical analysis, if not both as if you are unable to determine the current way the winds of the market are blowing then you will have no way of knowing if you are getting in ahead of the curve or simply following the crowd.

Ignoring the difference between implied and historical volatility: When trading options, implied volatility should be one of your main gauges when it comes to determining if the option in question is actually priced correctly. As a general rule, you can expect bearish markets to reflect higher amounts of implied volatility and naturally higher prices across the board. This does not mean it is al that you need to take into account, however, which is why historical volatility is important when it comes to choosing cheap options that are still going to end up being valuable in the long run. The historical volatility of the specific option can be found by first plotting it out beforehand as a means of determining the difference between general volatility and the volatility as it currently stands.

Ignoring probability: It is also important to keep in mind that the historical data does not, by nature, apply to current trends at all times which means it is important to take into account the probability in addition to the odds that the market is going to act in the way you can reasonably expect. The odds are how likely the market is going to behave as expected while the probability can be more accurately thought of as the likelihood of a given outcome. Understanding the importance of probability can make it easier to minimize the losses that can be found when it comes to less desirable underlying assets. When purchasing options on the cheap you are going to want to remember that they are never priced where they are as a fluke, which means you are going to need to choose wisely if you are going to beet the odds as doing otherwise is little more than gambling and there are betters ways to gamble than through options trading.

Not choosing parameters correctly: When it comes to choosing options surrounding front month contracts, it is crucial that you keep in mind the timeframe that relates to any expectations you may have for the underlying asset. While some options are always going to seem too good to be true, the truth is they are almost always hamstrung by a tight timeframe that is unlikely to pay off in the way you would hope as a result. Furthermore, regardless of the timeframe you choose, it is important to always maintain a realistic set of expectations when it comes to the movement you can expect from the underlying asset as it can still be significant even if the timeframe is limited.

Not comparing the intrinsic and extrinsic values: The extrinsic value is typically thought of as the difference between the price an option is currently going for, or possibly the inherent value based on any guaranteed premiums, even if it expires or the underlying asset experiences zero movement in the given timeframe. While the intrinsic value is always going to be considered when it comes to deciding which cheaper options are going to be worth considering, the extrinsic value becomes even more important as it decreases in value the closer the option is to its expiration date.

Underestimating commission costs: If you are hoping to develop a habit of trading cheaper options, then it is extremely important you ensure your broker already has an easy way to go about doing so before getting too deep into the planning process. A strategy that is based around cheap commissions is going to be one that is based around high risk and high reward which means that it will require a greater than an average number of trades in order to generate a successful trade percentage. As such, it would behoove you to ensure that you are paying for trades based on a percentage of the cost of the trade as opposed to a flat rate.

Not respecting stop losses: While placing a stop loss on a high-profile option is a non-brainer, many new traders make the mistake of not placing stop losses on all of their trades. Just because you are dealing with a less expensive option as a bevy of cheap losses can be just as detrimental as one, large loss. Whenever you are trading you should be thinking about the big picture which means minimizing your losses as much as possible, regardless of what is directly at stake. Failing to do so can lead to you burning through your trading capital far more quickly than you otherwise might.

Not taking advantage of the spread: New option traders typically get hung up when it comes on taking advantage of particularly volatile trades because they don't take into account the gains that can be accrued when using a spread to safeguard their trades. A long spread is created from two options, a call and a put, with all of the same relevant details, expiration date, amount and underlying stock. The only thing that will be different is the strike price. You will want to set the call at the higher strike price and the put at the lower strike price. This will ensure your losses don't exceed this point while also limiting your total profits to the difference between the two which makes it unfit for trends that you feel have unlimited potential in the short-term. Never commit to half a spread at a time as this provides the market opportunity to shift between the halves, skewing your potential for profit as a result.

Conclusion

Thank you for making it through to the end of Options Trading: How to Increase Your Income at Low Risk, let's hope it was informative and able to provide you with all of the tools you need to achieve your goals, whatever it is that they may be. Just because you've finished this book doesn't mean there is nothing left to learn on the topic, expanding your horizons is the only way to find the mastery you seek.

It is important to keep in mind that the market is always changing, as are the common techniques that traders use to capitalize on this fact, what this means is that if you truly hope to be successful as an options trader you will make a habit of being a lifelong learner and never resting on your laurels when it comes to gathering information about your chosen market. For now, however, it is time to stop reading and to start getting started practicing your options trading skills. Luckily, you can practice the basics without putting any money down by simply tracking your chosen underlying assets as well as their relevant options, making a decision on if you would buy or sell and then calculate your profits as if you had made the trade. While this won't get you used to the pressures of trading, it will help you understand the basics which is half the battle.

Finally, if you found this book useful in any way, a review on Amazon is always appreciated!

Description

While the financial realities of trading in the stock market mean that it is little more than a dream for most people, options trading is more affordable while still offer much of the overall potential for profit. If you're interested in learning more, then *Options Trading: How to Increase Your Income at Low Risk* is the book you are looking for.

While once only the domain of the Wall Street elite, the ready availability of the internet means that anyone can take advantage of this unique investment opportunity without shelling out big bucks for a traditional brokerage account. Inside, you will learn how you can get started today with as little as $1,000 and start on the road to a better tomorrow. So, what are you waiting for? Take control

www.ingramcontent.com/pod-product-compliance
Lightning Source LLC
Chambersburg PA
CBHW070208230526
45471CB00002B/875